South Yorkshire Collieries

on old picture postcards

Norman Ellis

1. Sinking of **Wath Colliery** began in 1873, the Barnsley bed being reached in 1876. In 1912 and 1923, the shafts were deepened to the Parkgate and Silkstone seams respectively. On this card of the colliery, postally used in 1906, coke ovens are just visible behind the wagons, right.

**Designed and Published by
Reflections of a Bygone Age,
Keyworth, Nottingham
1995**

Revised edition March 1999

+ Hemsworth   + Thorne
  (Fitzwilliam)   + Askern
                    + Upton
+ Monckton
          + South Kirkby   + Hatfield Main

          + Frickley   + Bullcroft
          (South Elmsall)
+ Monk Bretton
                                  + Brodsworth

                                      + Bentley
+ BARNSLEY
                    + Hickleton Main

      + Wombwell Main   + Barnborough

+ Barrow   + Wath
                                      + DONCASTER
+ Rockingham   + Denaby Main

      + Elsecar Main   + Cadeby Main

                              + Edlington
                              (Yorkshire Main)

                    + Dalton Main
                    (Silverwood)

      + ROTHERHAM   + Maltby

          + Rotherham Main
                              + Thurcroft
      + Tinsley Park

  + SHEFFIELD
                              + Dinnington
          + Birley East

SOUTH YORKSHIRE COLLIERIES

                    featured in this book

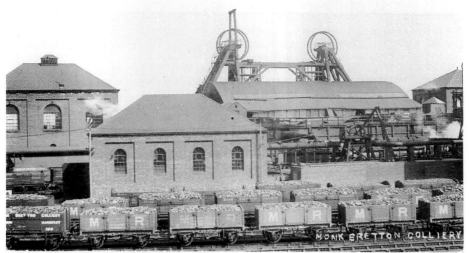

2. Monk Bretton Colliery was sunk about 1870. As depicted in the above view from early this century, the two headstocks and their engine houses (shown extreme left and right) were arranged in line. The headframes were braced together and partially enclosed. Midland Railway and colliery-owned trucks are visible.

Printed by
Adlard Print and Typesetting Services,
Ruddington, Notts.

ISBN 0 946245 98 3

Front cover: **Askern Colliery** on a card by E.L. Scrivens, Doncaster, postmarked Askern, 25th August 1930. *(see also illustrations 49 & 50).*
Back cover (top): The banner of the **Dearne Valley** branch of the Yorkshire Miners' Association, formed in 1881 from an amalgamation of the South Yorkshire and West Yorkshire Miners' Associations.
(bottom): **Hickleton Main Colliery,** where production commenced in 1894, on a card by Lamb of Barnsley, c.1912. *(see also illustration 22).*

INTRODUCTION

Coalmining in South Yorkshire was not just an occupation; more a way of life. When wholesale pit closures became evident, the distress was compounded because, not only would men lose their jobs, but communities would die.

Many South Yorkshire colliery villages were built or expanded for pit workers by colliery owners. Although the houses tended to be stereotyped, their overall standard compared favourably with other working class accommodation. Pit villages had their own shops, working men's clubs, welfare halls, and recreation grounds where cricket, rugby and bowls were played. Keeping pigeons or tending allotments were other leisure activities. Coal getting, being thirsty work, perhaps accounted for colliers liking their pint.

In some South Yorkshire villages, over 70% of men worked at the pit. The miners and their families were fiercely independent but ever willing to help each other. Lads carried few qualms about having to follow their dads down the pits.

Colliers carried a reputation, largely misplaced, for being obstructive. They battled for their birthright. A right to work, earn a decent wage and support their families. They complained little about the conditions which they endured down below. But theirs was ever a struggle against the machinations of politicians and pontificators.

The Yorkshire coalfield was continuous with the North Derbyshire and Nottinghamshire coalfields. The coal seams in Yorkshire dipped at a low angle from west to east and southeast.

In Yorkshire, outcrop coal was burned more than a thousand years ago. Later, horizontal tunnels (day holes) were driven into hillsides. The first vertical mines were bell pits. A shaft was dug downwards to the seam, then worked outwards to form the bell shape. When the working became unsafe, it was abandoned and another shaft dug.

Real expansion came in the late 18th century, mainly on the northwestern flank of the region, around Bradford, Halifax and Huddersfield. As the Industrial Revolution gained momentum, pits were also sunk in the Leeds and Wakefield areas. Coal was needed to raise steam in textile mills. Coke was required for iron smelting; coal gas for lighting. The railways stimulated trade by using and moving the coal.

From the 1840s, with the pioneering of new mining techniques, the South Yorkshire coalfield was gradually developed. At first, the Barnsley and Silkstone seams were exploited around Barnsley. Then, sinkings were made further east and south towards Rotherham and Doncaster, where the seams were much deeper. In the colliery time scale, many South Yorkshire pits were relative newcomers.

Landowners had rights to the minerals beneath their property. With some exceptions, collieries were worked upon leases, usually by registered companies. Whether company owned or privately owned, collieries were nationalised in January 1947, when the National Coal Board was formed.

The pictures in this book are from photographs which appeared on postcards during the first three decades of this century. The photographers and publishers concentrated on exterior shots, few interior ones being taken. Collieries, it seems, were as much a part of the landscape as churches, pubs or railway stations. The colliery headstocks, towering to the sky, had grace and elegance.

Norman Ellis
April 1995

3. Monckton Colliery, which originated in 1876, was situated east of Royston. New sinkings were made in the 1920s. After the colliery closed, Royston Drift Mine was opened on the same site, but this closed in 1989. The above card, published by J. Crowther Cox of Rotherham, was posted from Royston in 1909. It shows the screens and a ramshackle looking conveyor system.

4. Railway wagons laden with coal and pit props, including a Great Western truck, feature on this postcard of the pit yard at **Monckton Colliery,** c.1920. James L. Wood, its photographer, who lived in Midland Road, Royston, produced many photographs of the colliery.

Colliery Features

The surface configuration of each colliery varied according to its age, processes involved and methods of product disposal. Although the tall headstocks were a common feature, they showed diversification of design. Most collieries had a pair of them, situated above the downcast and upcast shafts respectively.

The large guide pulleys on the headstocks carried the drawing ropes from the vertical line of the shaft to a drum in the engine house. Coal was used to heat the boilers which raised steam to drive the engines, the smoke escaping up a tall chimney. The upright framework of the headstock was braced together and usually supported on one side by diagonal beams. Timber was used to construct early headframes, but was replaced by steel girder, steel lattice or reinforced concrete, wood becoming illegal in 1911.

Cages, some with two or three decks, were drawn up and down the shafts. Men were conveyed between pit top and bottom via the upcast shaft. Coal tubs were transported in the downcast shaft.

Coal, having been brought to the surface and taken to the screens, was sorted on conveyors by a series of screening or riddling actions into lumps, "nuts", slack, etc. Old men or boys were employed to extract the stone. Coal slack was sometimes used in the coke ovens or converted into briquettes. Coal sorting created a lot of waste which was generally conveyed by aerial ropeway to a tip. The huge dark tips, some sited near houses, became real eyesores.

A colliery surface complex also included a lamproom, offices, a laboratory, various conveyors and elevators, sidings for railway wagons, and facilities for "landsales" by road transport. Baths, canteens and medical centres were subsequent innovations.

Down the mine, methods of getting coal differed. Some collieries adopted pillar and stall working, where part of the coal was left standing as pillars to support the roof. This method was widely replaced by various types of longwall working, where miners worked together to extract coal from a length of face. Props and waste rock were used to support the roof.

Explosives were needed to break into the face of coal, followed by undercutting with a pick. Some men then hewed lumps of coal from the face with hammers and wedges; other men shovelled the coal into tubs or carried out roof maintenance. The gradual introduction of various types of mechanical coal cutters, which became ever more versatile, led to greater efficiency.

Coal was moved from face to shaft bottom by tubs or conveyors. The tubs were pulled by pit ponies or clipped on to an endless moving rope. Conveyors were also used from early this century. Underground locomotives for hauling tubs were introduced in the 1930s. Men walked from shaft bottom to coal face, sometimes several miles, until they were able to ride behind a loco or on a conveyor.

Added to the hard work were the less tangible rigours of working down the pit, such as the shift system, the threat of accidents and explosions, the diseases peculiar to the occupation and the animosity of some colliery owners. Through many of the struggles, colliers received backing from the Union.

5. Elsecar Main Colliery began production in 1908, taking coal from the Parkgate and, later, the Silkstone, Thorncliffe and Haigh Moor seams. Earl Fitzwilliam, the colliery's owner and the area's principal landowner, built nearly 150 houses at Elsecar for his workpeople. The screens are to the left on this card, published by E.L. Scrivens, Doncaster, and postmarked Barnsley, 7th September 1917.

6. Wombwell Main Colliery dated back to 1854, when the Barnsley seam was reached at 223 yards, later to be followed by the deeper Parkgate and Silkstone seams. It closed in 1969. The E.L. Scrivens postcard shows the colliery after installation of a washery complex beside the old screens, left of centre.

7. *"This is a postcard of the new pit which is being sunk not far from here, and the one which Walter will work at when finished."* The message was written by Bert Blott, who posted the card from Mexborough to his mother at West Byfleet, Surrey, on 18th November 1912. **Barnborough Colliery** became fully operational in 1915. Card published by Regina Co., Doncaster.

8. Barnborough Colliery (later known as Barnborough Main) rescue team, April 1929. The members proudly sport breathing apparatus around their necks; also kneecaps and lamps. Card produced by Medcarfs' Studio, Mexborough.

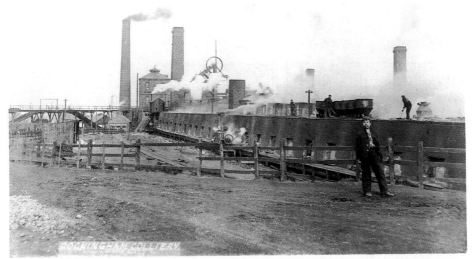

9. Rockingham Colliery, which belonged to Newton, Chambers & Co., was sunk near Worsborough in about 1875. It forms the backcloth on this card, postmarked Hoyland Common, 16th July 1907. Nearer the camera are the coking ovens, where coal slack was converted into coke.

10. Barnsley and Doncaster were favourite venues for the miners' demonstrations in South Yorkshire, which began in the mid 19th century. Highlight was the parade with bands and banners. The miners' procession on 17th June 1907 is shown descending Market Hill, **Barnsley.** Later in the day, Keir Hardie, visible in front of the parade, was chief speaker. The card, published by Denton & Co., Barnsley, was posted in the town on 21st June 1907.

NEW S. YORKS COAL FIELD.
1912 STRIKE. WARREN QUARRY LANE
BARNSLEY

11. In 1912, an estimated million miners went on strike nationwide to obtain a guaranteed minimum wage. The strike lasted from 1st March to mid-April. Coal picking from outcrops or pit heaps was widespread. Here, at an outcrop in Warren

Quarry Lane, on the south side of **Barnsley,** men, women and youngsters seem intent on finding their own black diamonds. Postcard published by Thomas Lamb of Barnsley.

12. Sinking of **Frickley Colliery,** South Elmsall, began in March 1903. As was often the case, the work was done by travelling sinkers, who moved to different assignments. The steel lattice construction of one of the two headstocks is clearly visible on this E.L. Scrivens view, which is postmarked 1925. Rather dramatically, the smoke and steam suggest that the winding engines were in use.

13. The first coal taken from the Barnsley bed at **Frickley Colliery** on 24th May 1905, on a printed postcard issued by James E. Winterburn, South Elmsall. The colliery closed in November 1993.

14. This photograph was taken 660 yards underground at **Frickley Colliery** in 1907. Not all areas at the pit bottom were as spacious as this. Observe the door and props. Various doors were opened and closed to control ventilation or permit passage of tubs. Card by J.E. Winterburn, South Elmsall.

15. In the 1870s, **Hemsworth Colliery** was constructed 1½ miles north of the village of Hemsworth at Fitzwilliam. The above view dates from 1926. Fitzwilliam and Kinsley (slightly nearer Hemsworth) evolved as colliery villages with much new housing.

16. *"Miners' houses and the coming generation of Reds. They don't appear to be behind in numbers."* So reads the handwriting on the reverse of this card, which shows pleasant new housing at Newstead Avenue, **Fitzwilliam.** This and the previous card were sold by John William Sutton at Fitzwilliam Post Office.

17. After the owners of Hemsworth Colliery pressed for substantial reductions in rates of pay in 1904-5, colliers withdrew their labour. They were ordered to vacate colliery-owned houses at Kinsley. Many families were evicted by police, some finding refuge in a hastily devised camp at **Kinsley,** shown above in August 1905.

18. Evicted miners had many sympathisers in **Kinsley.** The ballroom on the upper floor of the Kinsley Hotel was converted into sleeping quarters for children, pictured here at 6.00 a.m. on 30th August 1905. This and the preceding card were produced by Wales, photographer, Hemsworth.

19. Shortage of coal during the 1912 pit strike led to much illegal coal picking. Here, colliers are shown resting during pursuit of this activity near **Hemsworth Colliery.** On the back row, left, is Joseph Robinson, pit top boss and engineer, who should not have been with the strikers but was sympathetic to their cause.

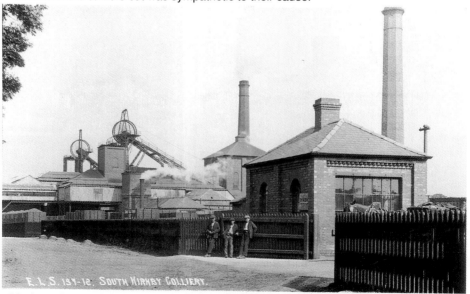

20. In 1876, work started on sinking two shafts for **South Kirkby Colliery.** The Barnsley seam was reached in 1878, later followed by the Haigh Moor seam. A horse and cart, of a type popularly used to deliver coal to householders, is partly visible, right, on this E.L.Scrivens postcard.

21. Upton Colliery had a shorter than average working life, the result of frequent bedevilment by geological faults and spontaneous combustion. Sinking began in 1924, the first coal was extracted in July 1927 and closure came in January 1966, although by then only the washery was operating. Card published by J. Simonton & Son, Balby, Doncaster.

22. Many collieries had a band, with players mainly recruited from the pit, at least in the early days. Cloth caps, mufflers and pit muck were swapped for smart uniforms. The prizewinning band of **Hickleton Main Colliery** was photographed in 1923.

Labels within image: T.COPE, C.ADAMS, T.W.JENNINGS, B, TOP OF SHAFT IN WHICH MEN WERE KILLED, DAMAGED LAMPS, DISASTER AT BA, SEVEN MEN (PHOTOGRAPHS AB, THE OTHER NINE OCCUPAN

23. Seven men were killed (pictured) when they were
Barrow Colliery, Worsborough, near Barnsley, on 15
Although not so credited, this commemorative card w
similar postcards of industrial disasters and railway acc

ISAAC FARRER   W GOODCHILD   FRANK DOBSON

...N COLLIERY NEAR BARNSLEY.   15ᵗʰ NOV 1907.

THROWN OUT OF CAGE AND INSTANTLY KILLED, FALLING A DEPTH OF 200 FT.

...RE OR LESS SERIOUSLY INJURED.

...om a double-decker cage to the bottom of the pit shaft at
...nber 1907. Nine other cage occupants received injuries.
...ork of Warner Gothard of Barnsley, who published many

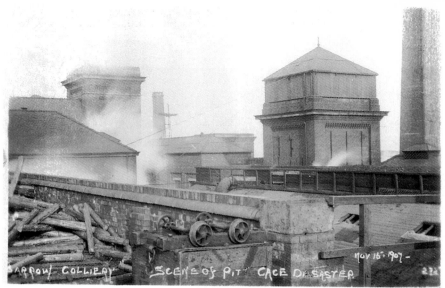

24. The unusually encased top of the shaft at **Barrow Colliery** down which the seven men fell, is shown here, right of centre. Notice the drawing ropes running down to an engine house, left. Barrow Colliery, which was sunk in 1875, closed after the 1984-5 miners' strike.

25. Rotherham Main Colliery at Canklow was sunk in 1890-3. The owners, John Brown & Co. Ltd., established a school at Canklow to take 145 children of their workpeople. The colliery was served by Rotherham Corporation trams, one of which is visible above. The card, published by M. Creswick, Wellgate, Rotherham, was posted from Maltby to Rotherham in 1907.

26. Shaft sinking for **Dalton Main Colliery,** near Thrybergh, began in 1900. Coal production commenced in 1905 after the Barnsley seam was reached. The colliery, also known as Silverwood, is shown shortly after opening. A pair of imposing lattice-framed headstocks is visible, together with one of the two engine houses and its boiler chimney, left.

27. A typical 12-ton capacity wooden railway wagon, owned by **Dalton Main Colliery.**

THE TINSLEY PARK COLLIERY COMPANY, Limited.

TINSLEY PARK

694

TINSLEY PARK

423

TI

PARKGATE PIT.

ROTARY PHOTO. E.C.

28. Tinsley Park Colliery, Sheffield, originated in about 1852, although deeper sinkings were made early this century, at which period the above headframe and gear were erected. The card, produced by Rotary Photographic Co., was issued by the colliery for advertising and correspondence purposes. The mine closed in 1943.

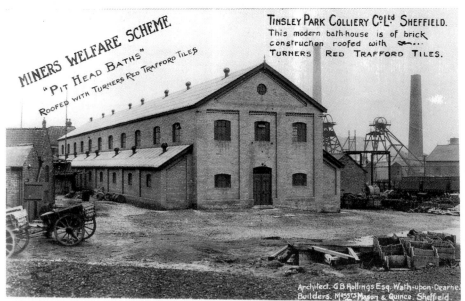

MINERS WELFARE SCHEME
"PIT HEAD BATHS"
ROOFED WITH TURNERS RED TRAFFORD TILES

TINSLEY PARK COLLIERY Co. Ltd SHEFFIELD.
This modern bath-house is of brick construction roofed with ⚬...
TURNERS RED TRAFFORD TILES.

Architect. G B Hollings Esq. Wath-upon-Dearne.
Builders. Messrs Mason & Quince. Sheffield.

29. Many colliers, arriving home with skins impregnated with coal dust, resorted to the tin bath, and water boiled over the fire or in the copper. From the 1920s, the Miners' Welfare Fund, financed by a levy on coal, provided pithead baths, canteens, clinics, etc. The **Tinsley Park Colliery** baths are shown on this publicity postcard. Turners were located at Trafford Park, Manchester.

No.1199. Coal Strike.1912.Poor digging for coal. Sheffield.

30. Digging for coal during the 1912 coal strike, somewhere in **Sheffield.** Poor people particularly needed coal for heating, cooking and washing. Postcard published by R. Sneath, Sheffield.

BIRLEY PIT. Nʀ WOODHOUSE 2188

31. South-east of Sheffield, the Sheffield Coal Co. established two collieries in the Birley area by the 1850s, known as Birley Vale and Birley West. A third, called **Birley East Colliery,** was sunk near Woodhouse in 1887-9. It is shown on a card published by R. Sneath, Sheffield, c.1912. The rural surroundings look disfigured by the pit waste tip.

59.2. Thurcroft Colliery. J.S.&S.

32. Thurcroft Colliery was sunk in 1909-13. The card, by J. Simonton & Son, Balby, Doncaster, was posted from Thurcroft by Joe Appleyard to his mother at Coningsby, Lincolnshire, on 15th October 1923. *"The X is over the boiler house where I do my bit of spare time."* At one period, over a third of Thurcroft's total population worked at the pit.

33. Sinking of **Dinnington Colliery** began in September 1902, coal being reached in August 1904, regarded as a record at the time. In the above view, postally used in 1909, a partially enclosed headstock, engine house and boiler chimney are visible. In 1908, Dinnington Colliery Co. built Dinnington Colliery Institute, with many recreational facilities. Card published by Taylor Bros. of Worksop.

34. Dinnington Miners' Welfare Football Club, 1928 season. Back row: J. Perry, —, W. Walton, W. Shone, W. Ford, G. Norbury, W. Webster. Front row: G. Selvey, A. Jenkins, B. Holmes, C. Merry, T. Probert, A. Muggleston, E. Probert. Postcard published by A. Seaman & Sons, Pinstone Street, Sheffield.

35. Sinking of **Bentley Colliery,** the first pit near Doncaster, was begun in October 1905. At the time, Arksey was the nearest village. The above view shows an early stage of the sinking, with a steam crane, navvies, piles of extracted dirt, a temporary trackway and a pile of bricks (probably for lining the shaft).

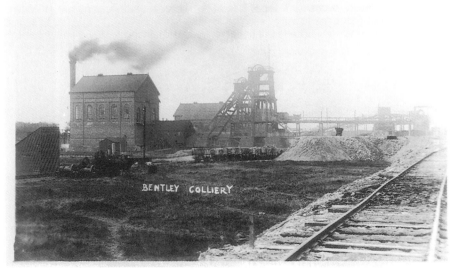

36. This card, postmarked 14th March 1909, shows **Bentley Colliery** prior to construction of some of the surface buildings. Coal production commenced during 1909. Bentley New Village, between the older Bentley and the colliery, was built to provide houses for the colliers.

37. This view of **Bentley Colliery,** from the opposite side, c.1912, shows the addition of more buildings. The headstock, left, was a replacement for one of the earlier headstocks. Its upper parts were steel girders, with reinforced concrete lower down. Postcard published by Regina Co., Doncaster.

38. Not the pond at **Bentley Colliery,** but floodwater, probably in 1932, on a card by L. Rice, photographer, Bentley.

39. Following the ceremony of cutting the first sod on 23rd October 1905, work began on sinking two shafts for **Brodsworth Colliery.** No.2 headgear is shown nearest camera and no.1 behind. With construction work incomplete, the area looks untidy. Note the lamppost, one of several on the site. The tall chimney belonged to the colliery's associated brickworks.

40. Brodsworth Colliery no.2 headstock and pit bank (i.e. the surface near the shaft where cages were loaded and unloaded). The headstock frames were in thick square-section timbers. Although the card is postmarked April 1911, it seems likely the photo was taken in late 1907 when Barnsley seam was reached. E.L. Scrivens produced this and the previous card.

41. Sinking of **Bullcroft Main Colliery,** at the edge of the village of Carcroft, commenced in 1908. After difficulties with inrushes of water, coal was reached in late 1911. The colliery, with a near-identical pair of lattice steel headstocks, is pictured shortly after opening.

42. Shown under construction in 1912, the new colliery village of **Bullcroft,** which now forms part of Carcroft.

43. Sinking of two shafts for **Denaby Main Colliery** began in 1863. Several coal measures were passed before the Barnsley seam was reached in 1867. It was a satisfying nine feet thick. The colliery is shown from where a level crossing took Doncaster Road over the Great Central Railway line, on a card posted from Denaby Main in 1914.

44. Most of the houses and other properties in the village of **Denaby Main** were owned by the colliery, even the "Denaby Main Hotel" on Doncaster Road, shown above, centre. It was built by the colliery company, which also appointed the landlord. Handily, the pawnbroker was situated opposite, with another one down the road. Card by R.J. Rosser.

45. Denaby Main Colliery Co. Ltd. started the sinking of nearby **Cadeby Main Colliery** in 1889, reaching the Barnsley seam in 1893. The company name became Denaby & Cadeby Main Colliery Co. Ltd. This card, posted in 1909, shows no.1 (downcast) shaft, right, and no.2 (upcast) shaft, left. Laden trucks are visible, right, having emerged from under the screening plant in the long building.

46. A stark statistic resulting from the disaster at **Cadeby Main Colliery** on 9th July 1912 was: 63 widows, 132 fatherless children. There were two underground explosions. The first blast killed 35 men; the second killed 53 men who were attempting to reach those hurt or killed in the first explosion. The agonising wait for news was captured on this card by Regina Co., Doncaster.

47. The 1912 pit strike was about minimum rates of pay, particularly for working in narrow seams where difficult conditions meant that less coal was hewed and less money earned. These strikers at **Cadeby Main Colliery** managed to put on a good face. This colliery closed in 1987, 19 years after sister pit Denaby Main.

48. Sinking of **Edlington Colliery** began in 1909. The Barnsley seam was reached at a (then) record depth of 905 yards in July 1911. The name was changed to Yorkshire Main Colliery. The colliery and new village are pictured in an agricultural setting on a card published by Regina Co., Doncaster. The pit owners provided the village with an open-air swimming bath in 1922.

Askern Pit. No. 1196.

49. The spa status of Askern took a tumble when, in December 1911, sinking commenced for **Askern Colliery.** The Barnsley bed, at 568 yards, was reached in a record 9 months. A spate of new housebuilding followed, which resulted in a much enlarged township. The colliery headstocks, engine houses and boiler complex are shown on a card issued by C. & A.G. Lewis of Nottingham shortly after the pit was opened.

ENGINE HOUSE Nº1 ASKERN COLLIERY

50. The winding engine in the no.1 engine house of **Askern Colliery** looks in impeccable condition on this card by William Bramley of Cross Gates, Leeds, posted from Askern on 14th July 1920.

Maltby Colliery 2.8.46

51. Maltby Colliery was sunk in 1908-10. *"I am sending you a photo of our pit. You will see it is a big place. Fifty men can go down and fifty men up, so that is 100 men in the shaft at once."* So wrote Don (who was residing at 39 Victoria Street, Maltby) on the back of the card, which was sent to Kitty (presumably his wife). The colliery had a history of excessive methane (firedamp) emissions. Postcard published by J. Simonton & Son, Balby, Doncaster.

52. The colliery company built an estate of 1000 houses in Maltby for workpeople at **Maltby Colliery,** which became renowned for its high production. Part of the screening plant is shown above, c.1912, on a card by Regina Co., Doncaster.

53. Sinking operations for **Hatfield Main Colliery** began in January 1912. Temporary headgear for shaft sinking is depicted on this card, postmarked Thorne, 12th August 1917. Observe the large bucket (known as a kibble) in the centre, for bringing out dirt. The slabs, each with one curved surface, were probably used to line the inside of the shaft. Card by Regina Co., Doncaster.

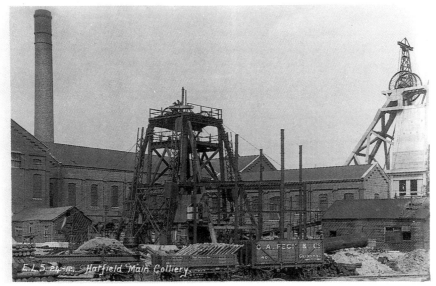

54. Some coal was raised at **Hatfield Main Colliery** using temporary headgear, but permanent headstocks were not completed until 1921. Uniquely, this E.L. Scrivens card shows assembly of a permanent lattice steel headframe around the earlier wooden frame, also shown in the previous view. Men are working on top. The concrete upcast shaft headstock, right, looks complete.

55. The smoking boiler chimney and apparently completed headstocks suggest that **Hatfield Main Colliery** had already started production when this photograph was taken. The colliery was near Stainforth, hence the alternative name.